"Shit-Hole Countries

By LaTim P. Onen and Shomari Onen

It is said that black people are prisoners of lamentations & sorrows...Let us not continue to blame God for what we can do ourselves.

Professor Patrick Loch Otieno Lumumba

CONTENTS

Lamentation of the Oppressed Child

I was born in the slums of the modern world

Yes, among warring gangs I was brought forth
from my mother's womb

In the middle of the Crips and the Blood gangs I
was born

From my mother's womb I was brought forth as
she fled from El Chapo Guzmán Loera.

Close to Trump's border wall I was born.

Separated & locked by ICE, I am

From the sprawling city of Venezuela, my
mother brought me into this world.

In Los Cabos, Mexico, the most dangerous city
in the world with a murder rate of 111.33 per
100,000 people, I was brought forth.

In Cape Town, a place of high crime,
unemployment rates and systemic racism, I was
brought forth by my mother.

In the poverty stricken cities of Latin America, I
was born.

Among bombed ruins of Syrian cities, I was brought forth.

Brought forth from my mother's womb I was born in the slums of Asia.

In the middle of conflict between the Israelis & Palestinians, I was born.

Born I was in a distant village of the African continent.

In the middle of the jungle I was born.

Among wild animals I was brought forth.

In the scorching heat of the world's desert, I was brought from my mother's womb.

Born I was in the middle of tribal wars.

War I was born in and is all I have known.

In my infancy I'm forced to carry guns.

Before I'm fully weaned from my mother's breasts, I am forced to carry guns.

Grown-ups force me to kill or be killed in their unending feuds.

They force me to do unthinkable deeds.

I'm forced to wander the cities, deserts, jungles, war-torn areas & wildness.

Serving grown-ups, I am forced to do or else.

These men are without shame doing unimaginable things with me.

Mistreated I'm by them, daily.

I'm left to fend for myself in this world.

In the inner cities & slums of the world I am forced to flee for my life.

Left alone to die in the jungles of the world, I am.

Riddled with scars and full of unimaginable maladies, is my body.

Slowly, I die from AIDS, cancer, hunger, malaria, & other maladies.

Fever ravages my body and soul but no one notices my plight.

From Flint, Michigan wells I drink poisoned water.

Cancer ravages my body from drinking poisoned water.

I drink dirty water from infested ponds of the world.

Worms fill my belly because I survive by drinking infested waters of the world.

Soon, the worms will consume & kill me.

Who will be there to save me from the worms in my belly?
Sores and scars cover my body because of the battles & near misses I have faced.
I'm driven from one place to another to wander in the wildness & jungles of the world.
Famished, I am kicked from one home after another.
The loaf of bread I long for is instead given to dogs.
Ashamed, I am naked & I roam the cities & jungles alone.
My relatives died because of poverty; there was not enough food to eat.
Survive, I must and I feel lucky because I made it alive one more day.
In my infancy, I'm tasked with the responsibility of raising the newly born.
I'm tasked with caring for the little ones whose folks died from HIV.
Pointless wars killed my parents & relatives.
Parentless and naked, I roam the streets & jungles
Concrete jungles I roam alone

Adornment and clothes are foreign to me
My skin is rough and my body is covered by
scars and calluses.
 Driven from place-to-place, normalcy is alien
to me.
Education & learning I will never know.
I will never know how it feels like sitting in a
classroom.
Books and writings are alien to me.
Daily, I face gun muzzles because of gang
menace & unnecessary wars.
 From infancy, war is all I have known and it
has become the norm for me.
 Taunting from other kids has become the norm
for me.
Daily, I witness senseless killing of relatives and
ordinary people.
 In school I should be but I will grow up without
education
 Because they turned me into a criminal at the
tender age of twelve, I live one day at a time.
I'm forced to do evil deeds because of
unnecessary wars and misguided adults.

They have turned me into a killing machine
because of their hatred for one another.

For their enjoyment, they force me to kill other
children.

These people are merciless and without
conscience.

Swift to judge, they are.

Swift to mistreat, they are.

Swift to drop bombs, they are.

Swift to inflict injustice, they are

Swift to kill, they are.

They are drunk from human blood.

Lives they value not.

Savages they are.

Like them, they have turned me into a savage.

I'm constantly running and hiding for fear of
what is done to me by grown-ups.

I'm left with no feeling and my childhood has
been deprived.

I'm haunted from watching the execution of
others.

They force upon me to drink concoctions to dull
my conscience.

I'm traumatized from doing and watching evil deeds committed by adults.

"Foreigner," they shout at me.
"Alien," they call me.
"What brings you here? Go back to where you came from," they yell at me.
They call me a foreigner because I do not look like one of them
At my tender age & innocence, they separate me from my siblings and hand me over to strangers who in turn have their way with me.
"Rapists, criminals," they shout at my kind.
"Go back from whence you came," they yell at me and spit in my face.
Who will save me from these heartless people?
Locked up, I am, for seeking a place of refuge.
They curse and spit in my face for no reason.
From place to place, they drive me
Running and surviving has become a part of me
Homeless, I sleep in hot asphalt
In the cold, I sleep.
Among concrete jungle, I curl up for comfort.

Among wild animals, I seek comfort & sleep.

Their furs are my blanket.

My breakfast and lunch are rotten leftover
carcasses

Rotten carcasses left by wild animals are my
diet.

Their urine and waste are my perfume.

The carcasses they leave behind are my meals.

Tomorrow I may become a meal to them.

For sanctuary, I run to the house of God

But the people of God drive me out.

Without shame, they chase me away.

Compassion for me, they have not.

Those who invite me in slyly, do so for personal
gain & to be used and abused.

I'm abused & used by so-called church elders.

Religious leaders use me to carry their greedy
and evil deeds.

Twisted and perverted, are their views of
religion.

They build mega worship places and fly in
private jets but the destitute, they jeer upon &
despise.

Mansions, they live in and luxury vehicles they parade gleefully.

"The Lord God is our savior and in Him we believe," they boast yet His commandments, they follow not

The poor and the widows, they turn away.

I'm used by politicians and the affluent to fulfill their own agendas.

Advantage, they take of my innocence.

Without shame, they sneak me in their abode for their enjoyment & indulgence.

These men are without shame, defiling the young & the innocent.

A pawn I have become, used by grown-ups.

Obey I must or face the consequences.

I face brutality and constant rape by those who are supposed to be my protectors.

I'm violated daily by them.

I live in constant fear for my life, fleeing from one place to the next I must.

Persecuted by them, I'm.

I'm locked up for speaking my mind

Inner Cities

My kinds and I are locked up in cells for no reason.
In order to make money, they lock us up.
In prisons, we must stay because there is none to fight our cause.
The ones who fought our cause, they silenced or murder.
My people are denied employment, jobless and penniless, we are.
To survive, we have been turned into robbers.
Preying upon one another, we must in order to survive the Caucasoid world, the Caucasoid dominance.
Abused and oppressed are my people, my very own people.
"You are a people from shithole", we are called unremorsefully.
"From shithole you came and to shithole you belong," they taunt my people.
These people are without shame, saying from "shithole" we came.

Is suffering all that there is to living in this world?

Will we live to see tomorrow?

Will we survive to see another dawn?

Will we ever know the tender touch of a mother?

A father's guidance, will we ever know what it is?

Will the world know of our plight?

Is there any hope for us?

Is there any hope for those like me?

Missing You

'I hope the person you are in love with does not make you sad at night.

I hope she is someone who will remind you how she loves you every day.

I hope she laughs at your jokes and listens to your music as I once did.

I hope she genuinely wants to be with you.

I hope she will not let you second guess her love for you.

I sincerely hope you find all the above because you really deserve the best.

I will always want the best for you even though we don't speak any more.

In my trials, I shall continue to love you.

Since she came into your life, I have no one else besides you.

Even though I cannot bear the thought of life without you, I must continue to live.

My mind cannot accept the fact that you don't love me anymore but survive, I must…

In her agony and solitude, she began to paint a picture.

A beautiful picture she painted.

The story of the picture she painted had a twist.

Her paint brush was a sharp razor.

The surface she painted on was her wrists.

Slowly but surely, she painted beautiful pictures on her arms.

The paints she made were crimson red...

Farewell

Be of good cheer…my love

But I must ask you…

Why are the autumn trees suddenly less
colorful?

Why is the summer sun a little less bright?

Why is the winter snow a little less whiter?

Why is springtime a little less beautiful?

Why is life a little less worth living?

Why is the starry night sky no longer blue?

Absent from you is the smile that used to greet
me, why?

Why? Why? Why?

Do not be sad that this had to happen.

I wish there was another way…

I did this because I wanted to.

Finally I will join the two other men in my life

Men who will not disappoint me, my late father
and brother who are in heaven.

My joyous life was turned upside down the day
the two were taken out of this world—happiness
turned into sadness.

The wonderful life I knew was never the same again…

That is, until you came into my life.

You gave me back what I had lost—happiness but most of all, love.

I did not know the meaning of love until I met you.

I did not know I would grow to love so much…

Life once more was worth living…

But somehow, along the way, the happiness and love you gave me was snatched away from me.

I lay in bed many a night sleepless—longing for love, your love.

I tried but was not able to bring back the joy and love you once gave me…somehow;

I was not able to bring back to you the smile that once radiated on your face

When you beheld me, the way your face lit up…

How can love be so sweet yet so bitter—so painful?

How can love break my heart so…?

Who is there to give comfort to my lonely, aching heart…?

Lonely nights

Cold bed

Eyes that cannot any longer cry

Eyes drained of tears…

Oh how so unbearable…

My heart longed to experience once more.

The joy we once shared.

Many a day I tried to keep it to together but my
strength failed me…

I tried to forget but the pain of not having you
beside me deprived me of peace.

The ever broken heart, tears, sleepless nights…

I never knew love would be so painful.

Will you miss me when I'm no more…?

Will your heart long for the love that was mine
to give you unrestrained?

Will you one day tell them…the children we
never had together… about you and me?

Will you show them my pictures?

The good times we shared

The jokes…laughter…

So many dreams not fulfilled…

So much life still to experience

Will you tell them?

I have learned that letting go is not easy

I know that being free is beautiful.

Life, somehow, mine must now come to an end.

Do not hate me or yourself…

I did this on my own.

I did this because I wanted to.

Do not blame yourself for any reason…this I did on my own will.

Till we meet again…in a better place

Where there is no sorrow

No broken hearts

No pain.

Remember my love for you

The love nobody living could give…

As much as I desired to give you

Yours forever in love…

Falling for You

Minding my own business, I was

I did not set out seeking for anything

But look, you showed up at my door

unannounced.

Now see what has happened to my heart!

What is this I feel for you that I have no right to

Why now?

My entire being is invaded but the

repercussions!

But surely, there is nothing between us.

So why the lonely and longing heart that make

me forget we are already taken by others?

You belong to another

I belonged to another but why this attraction?

Why this peace I feel when we are together?

Why this void I feel when you are not around?

Can a mistake feel this sweet and wonderful?

A mistake deserving no approval except from

our longing hearts

Can it be sweet yet so painful?

I never imagined we would come close to each other.

What is this I feel for you that my heart cannot explain?

Why the sudden yearning in my heart for you?

The Things You Do To Me...

"Oh the things you do to me…

The way you hold me…

The way you kiss and know me…

So firm yet so gentle.

Our hearts pulsating to the rhythm of

lovemaking…

What you do to my body, no one ever did

before.

I will love you till the end…

No matter what people think of us, my love is

for you and you alone.

I will love you forever…for eternity.

Take me away

Let us get lost in our own world

Our own…"

Becoming One with Thee...

"Behold, each time I open my eyes...

Beauty abounds around me.

Your splendor surrounds me

The majesty of your creations...

From the clouds above

Soothing breeze...

The cooling misty raindrops against my

exfoliating skin...

The beauty of the plants and blossoming

flowers...

Oh what delights to the sights!

Wandering birds in the sky abound

Insects and bees lazily buzzing in their unending

quests...

Pollinating flowers and bringing colors to the

world.

Diversity in nature, animal kingdom, glistering

ice...

Snowy mountains...

Endless flowing rivers and lakes

Blue sky and sparkling oceans

Vapors rising against the early

Rays of sunlight..

Oh what a sight to behold!

Soft and tender grass underneath my feet…

Dews that moisten and keep them alive

All for my delight…

 Oh how beautiful!

Sweet and melodious music of the birds and the
oceans…

 Melodies for my ears, my delights…

Morning birds above

 The sounds of animals

Small and big animals…

The purring of playful kittens

Cries of small babies seeking the comfort of
their mothers

Oh what magnificence!

What beauty to behold!

Oh how miraculous to hear the melodious
sounds

Sounds of many dialects…

Behold the different shades of humankind.

Surely, this lifetime allotted to me…

Timeframe on this earth

Beholding the beauties before me…

Will it be enough to enjoy the majestic

splendors?

Your handiwork…

Oh how mind blowing!

The deep blue sky

Starry nights, galaxies,

Pulsating quasars

Forming stars…

Dying stars beyond the distant horizon…

I come to unite as one…

The vastness of space…

 Beauties for me to behold and delight in

To wallow in…

The way, so long…

Time, so short…

The hurt, so unbearable…

Into your bosom I come…

Thy comfort, I seek…

Becoming one with thee

One with nature…

Bereavement of the Heart

'How do I tell the children that you are no
more?
How do I tell them that they will never lay eyes
on you again?
Please come back
Come back to them.
They are crying
Crying and waiting for you…
Can't take the pain…
Can't take the loss….
Please darling, don't leave me and the children
here on our own.
The world will be too lonely without you.
The road will be long and winding without you
Leave us not our own my love
Which path will lead us to you
To your comfort…
Why are you leaving us abruptly?
The children and I are waiting for you.
We keep waiting…

Hoping you will get better…

Hoping you will return home.

There was no sign you were leaving…

Departing us on our own, alone

I did not realize I would be without you…

Now I'm left here all alone and longing for you.

There will never be another to fill the void you
are leaving.

We are so right for one another

What will happen to me if you leave?

How can things go so wrong so suddenly?

What shall the children and I do now?

Please tell me that this is all a dream

A bad dream...

Tell me that this is not happening to you.

Will you go away and leave me alone?

Will you leave the children motherless?

What shall I tell them when they ask for you?

Who shall give them love if not you?

My love, how can this be?

Who will wipe away their tears?

Who will nurse them to health when they are
sick?

In the middle of the night when they are scared
and lonely, who will comfort them?
Lullaby, who will sing to them while tucking
them in bed?
Who will walk them to the park and show them
the animals?
There will be no meaning for life without you.
The sun will cease to shine . . .
The moon will no longer give its light.
The rain… the snow…
Who will play with them in the snow and rain?
Who will teach Junior how to make his first
snowman?
Life without you will have no meaning.
We keep waiting for you to come home
Darling… life has no more meaning.
It shall only be darkness for me
Only gloom if you walk away this day…
Sleep eludes my eyes…
Days and nights are long and unbearable
without you.
On that day you fell ill, seasons ceased…
Only darkness and gloom awaited me.
My eyes cannot cry any more…

They are drained from crying day and night.

Why did this have to happen to you?

Why did it have to happen to us?

Why break our hearts?

Why cause so much hurt?

I have been wrong before

I have taken my wrongs in stride…

Wrongs not meant for you, but it is your

absence how can I take it?

If you depart, how shall I get over you?

If you leave me, how shall I survive?

How do I survive without you?

I can take any loss but not this kind of loss.

I can take any blow but not this kind of blow

So much happiness you gave me…

Happiness I did not know before.

The children cry for you… for your love.

What shall I tell them?

How do I explain if you do not come back to

them?

If you are no more, how shall I tell them?

How shall I tell them that they shall no more lay

eyes on you?

That there shall be no more love for them from
you?
Who will love them more than you?
Cannot take the pain…
Cannot take the loss…

Africa, Africa, When Will You Wake Up?

And you men of renown, the rulers, politicians,
teachers, doctors, farmers, soldiers, fathers,
sons, brothers, uncles . . .
why do you fight?
Why are you swift to kill?
Is he not your father, brother, uncle, son,
daughter . . . that you fight and kill?
Is she not your mother, wife, daughter . . . the
one you rape, torture, and kill?
Are they not your neighbors and fellow
citizens?
Must you kill to show that you disagree with
them?
Can't you disagree without bloodshed?
Is your land not their land too?
Did you not struggle together for independence?
Did you not agree to build the land together as
brothers and sisters?
To enjoy the fruits thereof . . . ?

Whatever happened to the promises of self-rule,
self-governance?

Whatever became of dialogue?

Why do you behave in such a barbaric way?

Are you deficient of intellect?

Are others right when they call you barbaric,
beasts, savages . . . ?

Are you intellectually deficient?

Does not your behavior appall you?

Why is corruption rampant in your midst?

Why do you encourage corruption in your
midst?

Why do you cling to power?

Are others not fit to rule?

You have become the laughingstock of the
world

The butt of all jokes, you are

Yet in your ignorance, you proclaim yourself
civilized

You elevate yourself above reproach

"We are rich and powerful," you proclaim in
your vanity

You are delusional and ignorant . . .

Drawn in your own stupidity, you are . . . yet so
oblivious to it
You drain the treasury not belonging to you or
your family
The loot you deposit in foreign banks abroad
The country and the people you rule over are
left destitute
They have no means of providing for
themselves and their families
 In your vanity, you drain the treasury and
deposit the loot abroad
The people you rule over are unable to buy
basic necessities
They are dying from starvation, sickness,
unclean drinking water
Your children die from malnutrition
Those who survive, you imprison and enslave
The ones who dare ask, you subject to torture
You are like a depraved beast
A depraved beast is what you are
Killing, torturing, enslaving those who agree
with you not
No, you are worse than a depraved beast
You belong in chains, a slave you should be

So you can taste your own medicine

Slaves you are and slaves you will remain

Imprisoned in your own delusion, you are

Unless you wake up and join the rest of the

world, civilized world . . .

Beasts are incapable of reasoning

You are capable of reasoning but it eludes you

Who will save you from your depravity?

Who will save you from your insanity?

Who will make you see reason?

When will you wake up from your stupidity?

The world looks at you and laughs at you in

your delusion

They mock you and call you all kinds of names

Oblivious to the name-callings, you are

Oblivious to your own undoing, you are

Your actions justify the name-callings

You continue to behave the way you are called .

. .

Warring, killing, raping, inciting religious and

tribal cleansing . . .

In your delusion, you arm yourself to the teeth

You parade your feeble armament

Poverty abounds in the land

Children are starving

Citizens are dying from malnutrition

Why spend money in armament?

Who do you arm against?

By arming yourself, who do you intend to
defend against?

Where is the enemy?

Who is the enemy?

Which land has attacked you from without?

Who threatens you from across the seas?

And if they did, how will you defend yourselves
against them?

Will you fight them using the arms they sold
you?

Can you stand up against their might?

Surely he will smite you like a moth

He will annihilate you like annoying mosquitoes

In a single blow, he will erase you from the face
of this earth

Yet you exalt yourself in your vanity

You puff your chest in your vain delusion

You stand up in the international arena and
demand for equality

What a delusion, a delusion of unimaginable
proportion
Surely you will remain in your delusion and
perish in it
The weapons you buy you have turned against
your own people
Your own people you have turned against
Killing, raping, torturing your own people
Snuffing off the lives of the innocent
Defiling those who have known no sin
Depriving mothers of their loved ones
Terrorizing, plundering, encroaching . . .
Wicked heart you have...
Upon you be a million woes
May the blood of those you killed be upon you
and your children
May the wrath of the Lord befall you and your
children
May the wrath reserved for Lucifer awaits you
May you face the torments reserved for Lucifer
and his Angels...
May you imbibe the bitter pills reserved for him
and his Angels...

You bought into the lies fed you and turned
against your own people
You kill your own brothers and sisters
Your own children you drive from homes
The young and innocent, you rape and torture
Because you are not satisfied with killing the
ones you rule over, you turn to your neighboring
countries and incite violence
You jump in and declare war in the name of
defending the land
A delusional mind you have
A warring heart you carry
A fickle mind you were indeed endowed with
The laughingstock of the world!
When will you wake up?
When will you be proud of self?
When will you cherish self?
When will you stop killing your own?
And you, the innocent, when will you stand up?
When will you say "enough is enough?"
Did you not see the awakening in the land of the
pharaohs?
Now is your time
Time to wake up . . .

They Fight & Kill without a Cause

The sons of my people are in retreat

Pursued by a vengeful army . . .

They run without looking behind them

They run untiringly

They run for their lives . . .

The ones they once pursued now pursue them

The tide has now turned

It is now your turn to run

Left behind are wives and children

There is no time for harvest

Flee you must

There is no time to gather personal belongings

Belongings of value…

But run you must . . .

for dear lives, you must run

In close pursuit is the enemy

The one that once ran now chases you

You and your brothers must run for dear lives

There are rivers and mountains to cross

Yonder is a place of refuge . . .

A place to regroup and count the losses . . .

A place to lick wounds . . .

A place to make amends

Or is it a place to reassemble for counterattack?

Continue the fight . . .

Continue the circle of violence

Never-ending violence . . .

Your young are born in war and die in war

War is all they have known

War is what they will practice

The violence they were subjected to, they too
will do the same

Continuing the circle of violence . . .

Oh what a cursed people . . .

What a cursed race . . .

You will reap the reward of your actions

The cup you give to others will be given you

Warring among yourselves without end…

The women and the children are left behind

They suffer the unthinkable

Rape, torture, murder, they suffer . . .

But why do you now run?

And why do you seek a place to hide?

Did you not also rape and kill when you were in power?

You thought you were invincible then

Cries for mercy did not faze you then

Your eyes were bloodshot as you went about your business

Raping, killing . . . as if you were the very law of the land

Havoc you wrecked on your own people . . .

Mercy you did not show

Your deeds are now visited upon you and your household

The table has now turned on you

That which you wrought will now be visited upon you and your beloved

 It is now your turn to suffer and run . . .

Flee you must for your lives

The one you turned into an enemy has struck you and possessed your land

He has overtaken you and your land

Possessed, you have become

Powerless, you have become

Mercy shall not be shown upon you

Your children will see no mercy just as you did
not show one

Booties will your possessions become

You provoked him without provocation and
turned him into an enemy

Now he divides the spoils he has captured from
you

He ferries your women for himself . . .

Desolate is your home

A wasteland it has become

Your land has now become his land

He defiles your daughters and kills your sons

He rapes your wife and loots your town

Aflame is your town

Set on fire by him, your kindred

Dust and ashes is your town

Burnt to the ground are your houses

Your flocks, he takes away

He pursues you to the end of the earth

His sons sit in your town halls and laugh at your
plight

They laugh at your plight and the plight of your
children

He gathers your children and puts them in
squalid camps . . .
Under the pretense of protection, he forces them
in camps
"It is for their own good," he declares to the UN
representatives
"For their own protection . . . ," he tells the
world court
"The ones fleeing are terrorists," he declares
He taunts your wife and children asking,
"Where are your men now?"
"Who will protect you from us?" he mocks
"Who will protect you and your children from
us now?"
He unzips his trousers while smiling at your
wife and the wives of your kindred
Without shame, he takes her in front of the
children
Next in line are your young daughters . . .
The male child he then turns to, his lust is not
yet quenched . . .
Having satisfied his hedonistic carnal cravings,
he calls you and your beloved ones beasts,
cockroaches, savages . . .

He calls you a foreigner in your own land

He calls you enemy of the state

"I will squash you like an ant," he boasts

He commits infanticide

Genocide he commits as the world looks on

He promises to eliminate you and your kind

forgetting he is of the same kind

"Anyanya, terrorists," he calls you.

He promises to take pride in eliminating you

and your children

"Did your men not loot, rape, and kill us and our

children?" he taunts your wife and children

"Now it is our turn to return the favor," he

boasts and spits in their faces

He curses them and walks around your wife and

children pointing fingers

His eyes are bloodshot

He is ready to inflict more harm

Rape, loot, and shed blood, he will do

Your wife cries out for mercy

But who hears her cries?

Who hears her pleas for mercy?

Who will protect her from the tormentors?

Who will protect her children?

Her cries for mercy are in vain

Her pleas are in vain

Ignored by the world, she is…

Ignored by the world are her children…

Suffer at the hands of the tormentors, they must

Abandoned to their own fate, they are

He grabs your young daughters by the arm and

disappears around the corner . . .

Your wife hears screams and cries for help

Cries from her children…

Helpless, she is from the tormentors…

A gun is pointed at her and your children…

He and his buddies take turn at your daughters

There are more pleas and cries from your

daughters . . . but there is no stopping

There is no shame from them

Mercy is not forthcoming from them

"Oh God, where are you?" she cries out toward

the heavens

"Do you not see our plight?"

Are we not your children too?" she laments

One of them lashes at her

He strikes her down to shut her up

But she gets up and continues lamenting

She that came from her womb is being tortured,
raped . . . mercilessly

Your young sons are brutalized but she stands
there helpless

You are nowhere to be found . . .

Having fled in haste leaving them to fend for
themselves . . .

Your daughters scream for help and mercy

Your young sons beg for their lives

There is no mercy

Soon your sons lie bleeding on the ground . . .

Killed, killed for no reason.

Bullet riddled bodies lie on the ground

Innocent blood is shed . . .

Gunned down, they were . . .

Gunned for attempting to make a run from their
tormentors. . .

They were gunned down

They gunned them down in cold blood

They lies drowning in their own blood

The flesh from her womb lies dying before her
eyes . . .

In addition, screams from yonder is in the air

Screaming for help is your daughter

Defilers are upon her

They take turns in defiling her

"Anyanya, (terrorists)," they yell at her

She who is your wife is helpless

Cries from your daughter tear her heart to pieces

. . .

She loses all hope

It is a matter of time before they turn to her and

your other children

Your wife looks toward the heavens and prays

silently

She has lost all hope . . .

Hope from above . . .

Hope from humankind . . .

She lunges at one of them

But there is gunfire...

She winces in pain as she falls to the ground

The stench of lead ripping through flesh in the

air . . .

Lead ripping through innocent flesh . . .

She feels sharp pain tearing through her chest

She hears screams from your children, her

children

She is soaked in blood . . . her own blood

Darkness engulfs her

She falls on the ground

Finally, there is no pain

There is silence, darkness…

Void… a bottomless void . . .

 She is hurling toward a bottomless void . . .

Complete silence…

Complete absence of consciousness . . .

Peace, peace at last

No more torture…

No more suffering

No more . . .

3ʳᵈ World Groans

Dictators, why do you torment your people?

Yes, dictators around the world

Why do you mistreat your own people?

Should a mother not feed her young ones?

A mother should not have to feel the agony of

not being able to feed herself and her little ones

A mother does not have to endure the shame of

being raped in front of her children by

government soldiers

A mother does not have to feel the helplessness

of trying to raise her young ones in a country

torn by perpetual war, year in and year out

A war is a war, but there has to be cause to

fight a war

A mother does not have to see her children

slaughtered by the military because they do not

share the same view

A mother does not have to see her children die

slowly because she cannot afford medication

and/or feed them

A woman should not have to feel the pain of
her children dying from starvation because of
the inability to feed and nature them
A mother should not have to fend for her
children on her own because the government
took her husband away without just cause
A mother should not have to line up the whole
day for donated food because her own
government cannot provide for her and her
family
A mother does not have to exchange sex for
food in order to feed herself and the children
because her husband died in a senseless war
A mother does not have to watch the killing of
her children and husband because they belong to
a different tribe or clan
A mother should not be helpless because of
male domination
Motherhood should not happen at the age of
fifteen because society says so

Cries of the Innocent

There are cries from your people

 They cry out for help

They cry out to their own kind

"Kinsfolk, help me," ring out the cries

But your kinsfolk smiles and looks on

He knows of your plights

He sits in his palace ignoring your cries

He is in another country

In a neighboring country, he is

He sees your plight but looks the other way

He eats fine food and drinks expensive wine

He drives the most expensive automobiles

By air he travels with his concubines

He wines and dines

Spending lavishly from the treasury, is he

Treasury belonging to the people

He has many palaces and homes both nationally

and internationally

Dignitaries from foreign lands come to meet

with him

Expensive palaces he builds to entertain
dignitaries

Poverty stricken are his people

Yet he spends lavishly

Foolishly he spends

Dignitaries conduct business with him

They forge alliances and sign business contracts

There are oil fields to drill

Minerals to mine

Money to count

There is money to be made

Money to hide from the populace

The revenues from the oil and minerals he hides
from the populace

Only a small percentage he puts in the treasury

Some of it he shares with loyal friends, loyal
protectors

Protectors who will ensure he holds on to power

Power to enable more looting . . .

Looting and raping of the land, his land

The majority of the loot he puts in banks,
foreign banks

Some of the loot he will use for purchasing arms

Arms for protecting the country from imaginary
enemies . . .
All across the borders are people like him
Indeed, all across the continent are people like
him
But arms will be purchased anyway
Paleface will sell him the armaments
Yes, Paleface will sell Tar-man the arms
This way, Paleface can test the arms he invented
But you are oblivious to Paleface's intentions
Arms he sells you so that you can test them for
him.
Test them on your own kind.
He takes your money in return and promises you
more arms
You arm yourself to the teeth from an unknown
enemy
A figment of your imagination, you call enemies
There is in fact no enemy
The ones you imagine to be enemies are in fact,
your own kind
They speak like you and look like you
You went to the same school with them and
them with you.

You disagree with them from time to time but
they are no enemy
You and them are one, one race
You look like them and they look like you
The land and minerals belong to you both
Only language, religion, and boundaries
separate you from them
Yet you sit in your palace and laugh at their
plight
"That will never happen to me," you delude
yourself
"Let them handle their own problems. I have my
own," you contend
"Loot I will," you say in your heart
And loot you do
Oppress the people, you do
Arm a few to protect you, you do
Amass fortune, you do
You in your foolishness . . .
You in your vanity . . .
You in your . . .
Oh! When will it end?

Constant Failures & Regression

It is time to disperse the crowd and quell the riots

Election results are in question and there are rumors of vote rigging

Citizens are in uproar

Cities are on fire

People are dying

The people are counting on you

They count on you as a leader

A leader who should do the right thing, negotiate with the opponent

Negotiate to bring about peace and prosperity

The people are counting on you

But you, like the other leaders, refuse to strike a deal, a deal with the opposition

You cling onto power as if you are the only suitable leader

You understand and know there was vote rigging

You know the people are displeased with the results

You know there is a need for change

A change of heart, a change of attitudes, a change benefiting to all . . .

Yet you cling on to power, stubbornly

You look at Zimbabwe reassuringly, because you have similar interest

"I too will hold on to power as long as it takes," you say to yourself

The infrastructure of the country is beginning to crack

The economy is beginning to tumble

The people are restless

The people are tired of corruption, tyranny, dictatorship

They are tired of lining for hours for basic necessities

The old are weary

The young are restless

Potential investors are leaving

Cries for change are everywhere

Those close to you advise you to talk with the opposition

Prominent individuals ask you to talk with the
opposition
They advise you to have dialogue to avoid
violence wrecking the land
Like the people of your land, the people of the
continent, you refuse to hear
The violence and destruction continues
unabated
Innocent people die daily but you are unmoved
Foreign dignitaries call on you to have dialogue
but to no avail
Like the ruler before you, you refuse to budge
Ruling for life is the name of the game
regardless of how bad things are
Rule, you will because the army is behind you
Power is all that matters to your feeble mind
What will it take to open up your feeble mind, a
coup?
Can't that feeble mind understand that others
too must ascend to the rulership?
A cursed people, a cursed land indeed . . .
A people forever doomed to their own failures
and regression

The Promised Land?

And you in the Promised Land, why do you
fight your brother?
Why do you drive him from his land?
The land of his fathers and ancestors . . .
Does he not have a right to the land as you?
Why do you make him a sojourner in a strange
land?
Why do you drive him and his family to a land
where he is not wanted?
Were you not a sojourner once yourself?
When you were captured and taken to a foreign
land . . .
 Did you not call on your God & the God of
Abraham and plead your case?
When the enemy persecuted and killed you, did
you not cry out to Jehovah?
Did you not say to yourself, "Why does God
allow this?"
The enemy encircled you and had no mercy on
you
He did with you as he pleased

He had no shame, no compassion

He was like a depraved beast

He wanted your blood

He wanted your extinction

But God looked and had compassion

God remembered his covenant with your
forefathers

 He had mercy on you

He rescued your remnants from the wicked one.

Will you now do as the wicked?

Will you now uproot and scatter the inhabitants?

Will you visit on your brothers what was visited
upon you?

Will you not share the land that belongs to both
of you?

Will you forget that Jehovah heard your cry and
had compassion on you?

The people of the land cry out to God

He surely will hear their cries too

He is the son of your father, Abraham

He too has a right to the land

Jehovah will surely hear his cries just as he
heard and answered yours

So I beg you, sit and talk to your brother

The land is enough for both of you

You too, Ishmael, why do you seek to kill your
kindred Isaac?
Why do you deprive your brother of his
children?
Why do you hide his enemy among you, in your
midst?
The enemy attacks him and his children from
within your midst
They wrap themselves with explosives
They carry out hideous acts
Acts of cowardice . . .
Acts that kill the innocent
Will you not kick him who kills from your
midst?
You are a partaker of his evil deeds if you
conceal him in your midst
The one that is wounded and deprived of his
loved ones will come after the transgressor
Yes, he will come swiftly
He will come after you too
 For you hide his enemy in your midst

He will unleash his fury on you and your
children
Where will you run then?
To whom will you turn and plead your case?
To whom will you vent your frustration?
Who will help you?
First refuse him who hides among you
Refuse he who has evil intentions.
First reject him then plead your case
 For the land too is yours
It belongs to you and your kindred
Children of Abraham, you have disagreed long
enough
You have fought one another for far too long
It is time the children of the land live in peace
It is time fear is a thing of the past
Embrace one another
Share the new Capital
Jerusalem, the new Capital recognized by the
gentile
Share it with the descendants of Ismael
He is your brother and you are his brother
Stop the killing . . .

Stand up for one another and please your father,
Abraham

A Star among Us We Cherished Not

Born and raised among stars . . .

A star brighter than all, a shining star among us

You sang like an angel and danced like the devil

A star unlike any other

A star without equals

Beloved by many yet despised by others

Nonetheless, a star you were . . .

Much joy you brought to the world

Much happiness you bestowed upon us

Through your singing came awe-inspiring
melodies

The songs, dance moves, oh how inspiring!

We were awestruck by you

Awestruck by your singing

What blessings to us you were!

Yet we knew it not until you were gone

In a twinkling of an eye, you were gone.

Gone forever . . .

Because of you, we were the envy of the world

Many imitated but none could be like you
None can become like you because you were a
gift
A gift from above to us yet we found in our
hearts accusations
Accusations and the desire to malign your name
"He raped me," shouted some
"He molested me," others shouted
"A molester of children," some accused you
But you were found innocent
Innocent, you were found and acquitted
Now that you are no more, the vile resumes
The kind one, why did you leave so soon?
What was your hurry leaving us teary eyed?
The noble one, born and raised among the gifted
Why did you have to go so soon?
Legions mourn your departure
Born and raised among us with unique qualities
You were a star brighter than all others
When we beheld you in your infancy
We knew you were special among us
A star with few equals
You invoked in us awe
The melodies! Oh how sweet the melodies!

A voice like an angel's and those moves . . .

Oh how we were captivated by you

You sung like an angel and danced like the devil

Moonwalking all the way to our houses and hearts

How can we forget the night you shone like a star?

The night you first dazzled us with those moonwalks

We sat as if transfixed on our TV sets

No words, no sounds from us

Even our children stood still on their tracks, looking at you in awe and amazement

Looking at the masterpiece you executed that special night

When you were done, we wanted more…

And yet it was only the beginning

A beginning that transformed music and dance—forever…

We beheld you and fell in love...

You were like one of our own, a brother, a son, and even a father

Beloved by millions yet despised by many

You were dragged before a judge under false
accusations time and again
Smeared was your name under false accusations
Dignified even under much duress
You held your peace maintaining innocence
Your trials became our trials
Your troubles became our troubles
Silently we wept seeing how you were
mistreated
Our faiths, we maintained in you
Innocent! Innocent!
Innocence was declared yet others refused to
believe
Nonetheless, justice prevailed.
Beheld was the rule of law
Free, free we shouted—free at last…
Your joy became our joy
Your jubilation became our jubilation
Waited we did, for the day you would climb
back on stage
And what a joy when we heard you would be
back on stage
We held our breaths waiting
Waiting for that day you would return

Then came the sad news

The beloved one is no more

The beloved gloved one is no more...

The world stood still as if in disbelief

East, west, south, north... in disbelief

How could this be?

Why?

How?

Many questions arose

Who will be like you?

None! None!

Whose melodies will soothe our weary hearts?

Who will perform those moves?

Who will entertain us now that you are no
more?

Who will surpass the charitable works?

Imitators will spring up but none will be like
you

None will become like you

A gift you were to us from above

Yet we cherished you not

We found it in our hearts to accuse you

To accuse and malign your name

But now you are no more

You are gone

Gone forever

Gone too soon...

7.0 Magnitude

The fury of the earth . . .

The belching of the earth . . .

Explosive eruptions from within

Tragedy visited upon the land

Tragedy visited upon my brethren

The air is saturated with debris from the belly of

the earth

There is stench in the air

There is sulfur in the air

There is acid in the air

The smell of magma fills the air

Billowing from the belly of the earth is thick

and dark smoke

Poison from the center of the earth

From the skies fall dying birds

On the ground lies burning flesh

Lava burning the land and its inhabitants

Swallowed in the belly of the earth are homes

Valleys are flattened from the fury

Inundated are dwelling places

Dry lands have become wetlands

Displaced are inhabitants

Swallowed whole are once dwelling places

The children of the land die from starvation

The parched earth refuses to yield crops

Rain has ceased falling . . .

Sandstorm is upon the land

Tropical rainforests are afire

Aglow are the rainforests

Burning like inferno are the rainforests

What is becoming of the land?

Inundated from raging river are the lands

The glaciers give away its waters

Churning from within is the earth

Raging within is the earth

Gone amok is Nature unleashing its fury

Unleashing its fury on the land

Caught in the middle are lives

Who shall be left standing?

The fury directed upon us, who shall stop it?

The incessant fury of the earth…

Cries of agony beyond the hills

Lifeless bodies sprawled everywhere

Mountains and buildings tumble everywhere

There is stench in the air

Death is in the land

The Grimm Reaper is upon us

Visited, we are by the Grimm Reaper

Frail are the voices of the helpless

Frail from moaning their beloved

The eyes are sore, sore from crying

Tear ducts are drained empty

No more tears to be shed

Sleepless nights...

Fearful days...

Days of crying have emptied their tear ducts

We moan among our people

We moan and dry their tears

But they are inconsolable

We must cry with them

We must thirst with them

 We must hunger with them

The roofs of our bellies are in our backs

Hungry but no appetite

Like them, I have become as the son of Darfur...

Daughter of Mogadishu is what I have become

Father of the destitute is what I am

A mother of all woes I have become

Bereaved one of Fukushima Daiichi is who I am

A widow of Haiti earthquake I have become

Survivor of a Mississippi flooding is who I am

Survivor of mass shooting is what I have become

Sufferer of the world is what I have become

My days and nights are full of sorrows

My skin sticks to my bones

Thirsty but unable to drink

Hungry but unable to eat

Sorrowful but unable to cry anymore

My throat is perched

Sadness deprives me of sleep

Moaning keeps me up day and night

My limbs are sore from digging

Digging and moving rocks and boulders

Crushed are the bodies

Under the rock they breathe no more

Swept by raging floods, they were

Mowed down through senseless killing, they were

Burned in raging infernos, they were

Bombed to smithereens, they were

Overdosed, they were

Men, women, children; they are no more

Speechless, they are

Motionless, they are

Our work and good deeds must continue

Continue to bury those who are no more

Continue to make a difference

Continue to give a lending hand . . .

Darfur, Fallujah, Gulu, Harare, Mogadishu, DC . . .

Brothers and sisters, where are you?

Why war among yourselves?

Why have you turned the land into a killing field?

Why have you turned the land into a concentration camp?

Why do you separate children from their parents?

Why do you deny them refuge in the land?

Why call them, killers, rapists…?

And you Mogadishu…

Why is the land divided into clanships?

Are you not your brother's keeper?

Are you not your sister's keeper?

United Nations, I implore you…

Will you watch as I starve?

Will you watch and do nothing as nature overtakes me?

Will you do nothing as my people are raped?

I am driven from my land

Driven to a faraway land

Driven through the desert…

Penniless and without food or water

I must traverse the desert alone

Traverse the desert with my young ones

Heartless people pursue me

They overpower and do evil things to me

My clothes, they rip off

They have their way with me

I'm helpless before them

Guns are pointed at me and my children

Our cries they heed not

Our pleas they ignore

Our sorrow they shun

Bent on evil they are

Nothing will deter them

Nothing will hinder them

They spit and laugh at us

These people are without a heart

They are devoid of feelings

My child, they rip from my breasts

A knife is buried in the tender chest of my child

She would not stop crying

These people are merciless

They are without a heart

They are devoid of feelings

To the grave they send my precious little one

To the graves, they send the weaklings

To eternal sleep they send them

My cries they hear not

My pleas they ignore

My sorrows they shun

Pursued, I'm from my land

Who will protect me from them?

Who will rescue my young ones from them?

What will quench their thirsts for blood?

The desert sun taunts me

The mirage before me beckons me

My throat is parched

My tongue sticks to the roof of my throat

My children cry for milk

They cry for food

How shall I feed them?

Driven from my motherland, I'm

Driven from my birthplace, I'm

A wanderer I have become

I'm helpless

The world pays me no attention

The world looks away

They ignore my plight

Basking in their homes of retreat

Swirling expensive cool wine

Lying in the sun by the beach

Soaking in rays from above

Without a worry they are

I look to the sky, to the heavens

I cry out loud

But my cries are not heard

My cries are not answered

Ignored are my cries

Left to suffer alone, I am

Abandoned . . .

I must trek on

I must not lose hope

The stranger with a magic box approaches me

Snap, whirl, he records

He asks me questions

But his words I do not hear or understand

Speaking in a strange tongue . . .

Strange tongue, I do not understand

His pale skin burns in the desert sun

Must stop and rest my poor body

Must stop so the remaining child can rest

Must not lose this one . . .

A camp is before me

Bones protrude from my body

People stare at me and cross to the other side

They do not utter a word

Only their wondering eyes speak to me

The wondering eyes speak silently

The wondering eyes pierce my soul

"Why so emaciated?

"Why so bulimic?" their eyes ask

They do not understand my troubles

My many troubles they understand not

Those who know, care not for me and my child

Animals they compare me to

"Beasts," they call me and my young ones

My plights they do not understand

I lay awake at night—sleepless

I'm like a zombie in daylight

Food I have no appetite for

My life I despise

Why was I born?

Why did I not perish in the womb?

Why was I not snuffed off in infancy?

The Grimm Reaper, why did you spare me?

Afflictions are upon me

Will I suffer for the rest of my life?

Is this all that life has to offer?

Who shares in my plight?

And you, are you not my neighbor?

Are you not my keeper?

Why do you forsake me?

Why have you allowed my defilement?

Why did you not do something to protect my
beloved?

Why did they have to die?

Why was I not taken with them?

Why am I not counted among the dead?

Will I not rest alongside them?

Will I bury my beloved by myself?

Oh heavens!

Won't you dispatch me a helper?

Won't you ease my suffering?

Won't you quench my thirsts?

The tears in my eyes, won't you dry them?

Take me away from here

Away from constant pain

Away from constant tears

Away from never-ending flights

Away from constant heartbreak and
disappointment

Away from never-ending sadness

Away from defilement

Away from torment

Away from hunger

Away from never ending abuse

How much more torment must I endure?

How much more must I cry?

How much longer must I suffer?

My beloved lies lifeless in an earthquake

My brother is buried in a mudslide

My land was swept away by the raging tsunami

My sister breathed her last in the whirlwind of a
thunderstorm

My son was killed in a bomb blast

Domestic terrorists shot and killed my beloved

In a hail of gunfire he was mowed down

He was shattered to pieces from a terrorist's
bomb
My uncle did not return from the war
Perishing without a trace
A war unprovoked
A war provoked
Mindless, I have become from heartbreak and
loneliness
I'm all alone, a wanderer
Alone in an uncaring world
A world too busy to notice my sufferings
Heaven has forsaken me
Who will rescue me from my plight?
Who will comfort me in my loneliness?
My tears, who will wipe them?
In my distress, who will call upon me?
My brother's children, who will care for them?
Who will teach them righteousness now that he
is no more?
Love and virtue, which of you will show them?
My sister, who will fulfill her dreams?

Shit-Hole Countries

In your heart and your words, you say "Why are we having all these people from shithole countries come here?"

Why the crude language and off-color remarks?

Calling Haiti, El Salvador and some parts of Africa "shithole countries," why?

Why do you spark unprecedented international outrage?

Mr. President, did you forget that America's "greatness" was built on diversity?

Did you forget that your wives too came from other nations?

Did you forget that your forefathers too came from a distant land?

Mr. President, do you know why the countries you call "shitholes" are the way they are?

Did you forget that it is your kind who looted, raped and robbed those countries?

Have you forgotten that those same countries you call "shitholes" are that way because you continue to loot, rape and robe them?

Mr. President, you occupy the highest office in the world, have you no shame uttering disparaging words?

"Make America great again," you say but great again for who? For a select few?

Mr. President, is Hillary as crooked as you think and say she is?

Is she the most corrupt person to run for the presidency of the United States?

Does she suffer from bad judgement as you put it?

Does she only know how to make a speech when it is a hit on you?

Has she no policy?

You say she uses the oldest play in the Democratic playbook, is it true?

You also say she uses race-baiting, all talk and no action, is that a true statement, sir?

You also accuse her of "pandering to the worst instincts in our society and that she should be ashamed of herself, is that an accurate statement?"

Mr. President, sir, regarding CNN, you say "a total meltdown with their FAKE NEWS"

"Ratings are tanking since election, credibility will soon be gone!"

"They don't have a clue!"

"FAKE NEWS!"

"I thought that @CNN would get better after they failed so badly in their support of Hillary Clinton however, since election, they are worse!"

"They will never learn!"

"Fraud"

"Everyone knows they are biased"

"So negative"

"Really bad""

"CNN (Clinton News Network).

Mr. President, is Stephen Colbert, the Late Show host very weak and untalented, fighting over table scraps?

Will he be wacky in the unemployment line?

Was James Comey, the former FBI director a disgrace to the FBI?

Will he go down as the worse Director in its long and once proud history?

Was your firing of him a great day for America as you put it?

Mr. President, how about Ted Cruz?

Does he not have the right 'temperament' to be President?"

Is he "disloyal?"

Is he the "biggest liar in politics?"

Is he "a world class LIAR?"

"A true lowlife pol?"

Is he a "complete & total liar as well as a cheater?"

Does he "hold the Bible high and then lies and misrepresents the facts?"

Is he "Nasty?"

Does he really "LIE?"

And what do you say about S.E. Cupp (columnist)?

Is he a "flunkie?"

Is he "(one) of the dumbest people in politics?"

As you stated, is he "one of the least talented people on television?"

You say that he is "totally biased loser who doesn't have a clue, is it true?"

You also say that he is "hard to watch and has zero talent."

He is "one of the dumber pundits on tv, is that a presidential statement?"

You say that Bill de Blasio is "another beauty and the worse mayor in the U.S.", is that true?

You add that "if you like high taxes & crime, he's your man."

Is he truly "the worst Mayor in the history of New York City and has no imagination?"

You say that Robert De Niro is "a very Low IQ individual."

That he "has received too many shots to the head by real boxers in movies"

"I watched him last night and truly believe he may be 'punch-drunk,'" you added

You also said of columnist, Maureen Dowd, "Crazy and wacky."

That she "pretends she knows me well--wrong!"

"Makes up things that I never said, is boring interviews and column."

"A neurotic dope," you added about her.

What do you think of Erick Erickson, the conservative commentator?

Is it true that he "got fired like a dog from Red
State?"
Did he really "run the Red State into the ground?"
And is it true that he has "no 'it' factor?"
You say that he is a "total low life and
will fade fast," is that a fact?
You also added that he is "a major sleaze and
buffoon."

Mr. President, you say of ESPN: "it is no wonder
ESPN ratings have 'tanked,' in fact, tanked so badly
it is the talk of the industry!"
"People are dumping it in RECORD numbers, you
added," the last time I checked, people are not
dumping it.

Of Jimmy Fallon, you stated that "Whimpering to
all."
"Be a man Jimmy," you said of Jimmy.

Regarding experts on North Korea, you stated
"people who have failed for years."
"They got NOTHING, thanks anyway!"
"Failed fools," you gleefully added.

On Dianne Feinstein, a U.S Senator, you accused her as "Very disrespectful…"

In addition, you said of her as "Sneaky Dianne Feinstein, a disgrace."

On Jeff Flake (former Senator) you said: "Jeff Flake(y), unelectable in Arizona, doing a terrible job!"

You added that he was "A weak and ineffective guy, setting record low polling numbers."

You added that he was "humiliatingly forced out of his own Senate seat without even a fight."

You taunted him, "Had zero chance of being elected. Now act so hurt & wounded!"

"Not a fan, weak on crime & border…" you said of him.

"A total mess-big crime, going through massive attacks to its people by the migrants allowed to enter the country," you spoke of Germany, a friendly nation to us.

U.S Senator Kirsten Gillibrand did not get sympathetic words from you either when you stated that a: "Lightweight, a total flunky for Chuck Schumer"

"Someone who would come to my office 'begging' for campaign contributions not so long ago (and would do anything for them)," you said of him.

"Very disloyal," yet you added of him.

Regarding former candidate for Florida governor, Andrew Gillum, "If Andrew Gillum did the same job with Florida that he has done in Tallahassee as Mayor, the State will be a crime ridden, overtaxed mess, a thief."

Of him you said, "Presides over one of the worst run, and most corrupt, cities in Florida."

"Will make Florida the next Venezuela, runs one of the worst & most corrupt cities in USA."

Harsh words Mr. President when you said that he is "a failed Socialist, a Mayor who allowed crime & many other problems to flourish in his city."

Google, you did not spare: "Sooo on the side of the Radical Left Democrats, helping China and their military, but not the U.S.. Terrible!"

You also said the company is "so biased toward the Dems it is ridiculous!"

"Very dangerous, suppressing voices of Conservatives and hiding information and news that is good, controlling what we can & cannot see," you stated of the company.

On Senator Lindsey Graham, you stated: "So hard to believe that Lindsey Graham would be against saving soldier lives & billions of $$$"

"Publicity seeking"

"Falsely stated that I said there is moral equivalency between the KKK, neo-Nazis & white supremacists"

"A disgusting lie"

"Just can't forget his election trouncing"

"Always looking to start World War III"

"Sadly weak on immigration"

"Really sad"

"No honor!"

"I ran him out of the race like a little boy"

"In the end he had no support"

"ALL TALK AND NO ACTION!"

"Failed presidential candidate"

"Should respect me"

"Nasty!"

"Dumb mouthpiece"

"Got zero against me- no cred!"

"Had zero in his presidential run before dropping out in disgrace"

"Embarrassed himself with his failed run for President"

"Embarrasses himself with endorsement of Bush"

"So easy to beat!"

Wow! Those were strong words Mr. President.

On Guatemala & Honduras: "taking U.S. money for years, and doing ABSOLUTELY NOTHING for us"

"All talk and no action"

"They have taken our money for years, and do Nothing"

"Doing nothing for the United States but taking our money"

"Leaders are doing little"

On Maggie Haberman, the New York Times reporter: "a third rate reporter"

"A Crooked Hillary flunkie who I don't speak to and have nothing to do with"
"A Hillary flunky"
"Knows nothing about me and is not given access"
"Third-rate-reporter"
"Totally in the Hillary circle of bias"
"Sad"

The Political reporter, Mark Halperin, you stated:
"Sleepy Eyes"
"Doesn't have a natural instinct for politics"

On Health insurance individual mandate: "very unfair and unpopular"
"Highly unpopular"
"The most hated part of Obama Care"
"Terrible"
"Very unfair"
"Unpopular"

On the Associated Press reporter Jeff Horwitz:
 "one of the worst reporters in the business"
"Wouldn't know the truth if it hit him in the face"

Regarding the Investigations of the Trump
presidency you stated:

"Witch Hunt!"

"The greatest Witch Hunt in political history"

"Sad!"

"A big Dem HOAX!"

"A big Dem scam"

"Distraction"

"Witch Hunt"

"Witch Hunt"

"The single greatest WITCH HUNT in American
political history"

Regarding Iran, you said a mouthful:

"the world's leading state sponsor of terror"

"Responsible for backing Animal Assad"

"Corrupt government"

"Corrupt and poorly run country"

"Not good!"

"Playing with fire"

"They don't appreciate how kind President Obama
was to them. Not me!"

"Has been formally PUT ON NOTICE"

"Should have been thankful for the terrible deal the U.S. made with them!"

"Doing many bad things behind our backs"

Regarding the Iran Nuclear Deal:

"horrific"

"Horrible"

"It was all a big lie"

"Bad"

"Defective at its core"

"Not much of an agreement we have!"

"Horribly negotiated"

"Really sad!"

"Truly stupid"

"Insane"

"Incompetent"

"One of the most incompetent ever made"

"Is a catastrophe"

"Will lead to at least partial world destruction"

"One of the dumbest & most dangerous misjudgments ever"

"Poses a direct national security threat"

On Islamic State:

"they are losers and barely breathing"

"Low-level degenerates"

"Thugs"

"Losers"

Regarding actor Samuel L. Jackson:

"Don't like Samuel Jackson's golf swing. Not athletic"

"Cheats"

"Does too many TV commercials – boring"

"Not a fan"

On G.O.P consultant, Cheri Jacobus:

"really dumb"

"Begged my people for a job"

"Major loser, zero credibility!"

"Went hostile"

"A real dummy"

"Virtually incompetent"

"Failed career"

"Incoherent with anger"

Regarding LeBron James:

"LeBron James was just interviewed by the dumbest man on television, Don Lemon. He made LeBron look smart, which isn't easy to do. I like Mike!"

Regarding performer Penn Jillette:

"Sad"

"Worst show in Las Vegas"

"Hokey garbage"

"Goofball atheist"

"Never had a chance"

"Wrote letter to me begging for forgiveness"

"Boring guy"

Regarding the leader of North Korea Kim Jong-un:

"Will someone from his depleted and food starved regime please inform him that I too have a Nuclear Button"

"Little Rocket Man"

"I would NEVER call him 'short and fat'"

"Little Rocket Man"

"Rocket Man"

"Little Rocket Man"

"Obviously a madman"

"Rocket Man"

On North Korea:

"a rogue nation"

"A great threat and embarrassment to China"

"They only understand one thing"

"U.S. has been talking to North Korea, and paying
them extortion money, for 25 years"

"Has shown great disrespect for their neighbor,
China"

"Bad!"

"Looking for trouble"

Regarding Ohio Governor John Kasich:

"very unpopular"

"Failed presidential candidate"

"Typical politician"

"Can't make a deal work"

"Mathematically dead and totally desperate"

"Will drop like a rock in the polls"

"Only looks O.K. in polls against Hillary because nobody views him as a threat and therefore have placed ZERO negative ads against him"

"Bought and paid for by lobbyists!"

"Absentee Governor"

"Good for Mexico!"

"Doesn't have what it takes"

"Can't debate"

"Dummy"

"One of the worst presidential candidates in history"

"So easy to beat!"

"Total failure"

"Total dud"

"Fell right into President Obama's trap on Obama Care"

"I will sue him just for fun!"

"So irrelevant to the race"

"Pathetic"

"Failed image"

"Failed campaign & debating skills"

"Wasting time & money"

Regarding former Fox News anchor Megan Kelly:

"You have no idea what my strategy on ISIS is"

"Get your facts straight"

"BAD"

"Highly overrated"

"So average in so many ways!"

"Crazy"

"Never worth watching"

"Sick"

"The most overrated person on tv"

"Highly overrated"

"Is always complaining about Trump and yet she devotes her shows to me"

"Crazy"

"Her bad show is a total hit piece on me"

"Crazy"

"Can't watch Crazy Megan anymore"

"Without me her ratings would tank"

"Get a life Megan!"

"Lightweight reporter"

"I refuse to call Megan Kelly a bimbo, because that would not be politically correct"

"So average in every way"

"Dopey"

"Lies"

"Highly overrated"

"Very bad at math"

"The most overrated anchor"

"Really weird, she's being driven crazy"

"Had her two puppets say bad stuff"

"Should take another eleven day 'unscheduled' vacation"

"Really off her game"

"Not very good or professional"

About Jimmy Kimmel:

"very weak and untalented"

"Fighting over table scraps"

"Will be wacky in the unemployment line"

Regarding the Koch brothers:

"globalist"

"Have become a total joke"

"Are against Strong Borders and Powerful Trade"

"I don't need their money or bad ideas"

"Their network is highly overrated"

"I have beaten them at every turn"

"Two nice guys with bad ideas"

About late night talk shows:

"not funny/no talent"

"Spend all of their time knocking the same person (me), over & over, without so much of a mention of "the other side""

"An advertisement without consequences"

"The one-sided hatred"

"Unwatchable"

Regarding CNN anchor Don Lemon:

"the dumbest man on television"

"The dumbest man on television"

"I never watch Don Lemon, who I once called the 'dumbest man on television!'"

"A lightweight"

"Dumb as a rock"

On U.S. Congressman John Lewis:

"All talk, talk, and talk - no action or results"

"Sad!"

"Should spend more time on fixing and helping his district, which is in horrible shape and falling apart"

On National Review editor, Rich Lowry:

"clueless"

"Incompetent"

"Should not be allowed on TV"

"Truly one of the dumbest of the talking heads"

"Doesn't have a clue!"

Regarding Political Consultant, Frank Luntz:

"a total clown"

"A clown"

"Where did you find that dumb panel"

"A low-class slob"

"Knows nothing about me or my religion"

"Came to my office looking for work"

Regarding the Main Stream Media:

"The mainstream" media

"Fake News Media"

"Fake & Corrupt Press!"

"Has never been as corrupt and deranged as it is today"

"The true ENEMY OF THE PEOPLE!"

"They refuse to cover the REAL Russia Hoax"

"Always uses unnamed sources (because their sources don't even exist)"

"Fake News"

"Whose bias & dishonesty is greater than ever"

"Fake News"

"Every question is asked in the most negative way"

"Should be ashamed"

"The USA is wise to your game of dishonesty and deception!"

"Fraudulent and highly inaccurate coverage of Iran"

"Highly inaccurate Fake News hit job!"

"Radical Left Wing"

"Knowingly getting the Russia Collusion Delusion story so wrong"

"Much of what they do is FAKE NEWS!"

"Today I have, as President, perhaps the greatest economy in history...and to the Mainstream Media, it means NOTHING"

"Doing everything possible to stir up and anger the pols"

"Corrupt and getting worse, if that is possible, every day!"

"Has never been more inaccurate or corrupt than it is today"

"It only seems to get worse"

"So much Fake News...!"

On Omarosa Manigault:

(former Trump Aide), "Wacky"

"Deranged"

"A crazed, crying lowlife"

"That dog!"

"Wacky Omarosa"

"Got fired 3 times on the Apprentice, now got fired for the last time"

"She never made it, never will"

"Begged me for a job, tears in her eyes"

"People in the White House hated her"

"Vicious, but not smart"

"Heard really bad things"

"Nasty to people & would constantly miss meetings & work"

"A loser"

"Nothing but problems"

"A lowlife"

"Wacky"

"Wacky Omarosa"

"She never made it, never will"

"Begged me for a job, tears in her eyes"

"People in the White House hated her, vicious, but not smart"

On former FBI Deputy Director, Andrew McCabe:

"now disgraced"

"Didn't go to the bathroom without the approval of Leakin' James Comey!"

"I never called his wife a loser to him (another McCabe made up lie)!"

"So many lies"

"Disgraced"

"Now his story gets even more deranged"

"Disgraced"

"Pretends to be a 'poor little Angel' when in fact he was a big part of the Crooked Hillary Scandal"

"A puppet"

"A disgrace to the FBI and a disgrace to our Country"

"Bad! so-called 'leader'"

"Corrupt"

"Disgraced"

"Loser"

"Lies to Congress"

"Clown"

"Poor leadership"

"Committed many crimes!"

"A total disaster"

"He LIED! LIED! LIED!"

"Was totally controlled by Comey"

"McCabe is Comey!!"

"I don't believe he made memos except to help his own agenda"

"Andrew McCabe FIRED, a great day for the hard working men and women of the FBI"

"He knew all about the lies and corruption going on at the highest levels of the FBI!"

"A Comey friend"

"Got big dollars ($700,000) for his wife's political run from Hillary Clinton"

"Got $700,000 from H for wife!"

Regarding the late U.S. Senator, John McCain:

"last in his class"

"Sent the Fake Dossier to the FBI and Media hoping to have it printed BEFORE the Election"

"Failed (as usual)"

"He had far worse 'stains' than this"

"My oh my has he changed-complete turn from years of talk!"

"Never had any intention of voting for this Bill"

"Let Arizona down!"

"Let his best friend L.G. down!"

"He's been losing so long he doesn't know how to win anymore"

"Always looking to start World War III"

"Sadly weak on immigration"

"Very foul mouthed"

"Begged for my support during his primary (I gave, he won)"

"Has done nothing"

"I am no fan"

"All he does is go on television is talk, talk, talk"

"Incapable of doing anything."

"Has failed miserably"

"Doing a lousy job in taking care of our Vets"

"Let us down"

"Dummy"

"Graduated last in his class"

"Should be defeated in the primaries"

On Mexico:

"doing NOTHING to stop the Caravan"

"Has a massive crime problem"

"Is doing little to help!"

"Doing very little, if not NOTHING, at stopping people from flowing into Mexico through their Southern Border"

"They must stop the big drug and people flows, or I will stop their cash cow, NAFTA"

"The number one most dangerous country in the world"

"Just ranked the second deadliest country in the world"

"Totally corrupt gov't"

"Totally corrupt"

"We get the killers, drugs & crime, they get the money!"

"Unbelievable corruption"

"Not our friend"

"They're killing us"

On "Morning Joe" (Television Show):

"A really bad show with low ratings - and will only get worse"

"Ratings for "Morning Joe" which were really bad in the first place, just "tanked" with the release of the Mueller Report"

"Terrible ratings"

"A dead show with very few people watching"

"FAKE NEWS, Bad show"

"Poorly rated"

"Don't watch anymore"

"Low ratings"

"Unwatchable!"

"Sad & irrelevant!"

"Little watched"

"Nobody is watching"

"Gone off the deep end"

"Bad ratings"

"Small audience"

"Low ratings!"

"They misrepresent my positions!"

"Rapidly fading"

"Off the rails"

"Waste of time"

On MSNBC:

"T.V. ratings of CNN & MSNBC tanked last night"

"Trump Haters"

"Fake"

"Fake"

"A total joke"

"Bad ratings"

"Got scammed when they covered the anti-Trump Russia rally wall-to-wall"

"They probably knew it was Fake News but, because it was a rally against me, they pushed it hard anyway"

"Really dishonest newscasters"

"I seldom, if ever, watch"

"Fake News"

"Unwatchable"

Regarding Robert Mueller:

"a Trump hater who was highly conflicted"

"Big time conflicts of interest"

"A rogue and out of control prosecutor"

"A much different man than people think"

"Refuses to look at the real crimes on the other side"

"A conflicted prosecutor gone rogue"

"Only looking at one side, not the other"

"The Fake News Media builds Bob Mueller up as a Saint, when in actuality he is the exact opposite"

"Doing TREMENDOUS damage to our
Criminal Justice System"
"He is only looking at one side and not the
other"
"Will he be covering all of his conflicts of
interest in a preamble"
"Highly conflicted"
"Highly conflicted (and NOT Senate approved)"
"Why is he protecting Crooked Hillary, Comey,
McCabe, Lisa Page & her lover, Peter S, and all
of his friends on the other side?"
"Highly conflicted"
"Disgraced and discredited"
"Just someone looking for trouble"
"Heavily conflicted"
"Only appointing Angry Dems"
"Comey's best friend"
"Most conflicted of all"
On Members of Robert Mueller's team,
"18 Angry Trump-Hating Democrats"
"18 Angry Dems who hated Trump"
"18 VERY ANGRY Democrats"
"Trump Haters and Angry Democrats"
"Were devastated by the No Collusion finding!"

"Written as nastily as possible by 13 (18) Angry Democrats"

"18 Angry Democrats who also happen to be Trump Haters (and Clinton Supporters)"

"Illegally leaking information to the press"

"Investigating an event that never happened"

"Some very bad, conflicted & corrupt people"

The Mueller Report:

"A total "hit job""

"Should never have been allowed to start in the first place!"

"Should not have been authorized in the first place"

"Crazy"

"A big, fat, waste of time, energy and money"

Regarding N.F.L. players who kneel before the national anthem:

"Weak and out of control!"

"Showing total disrespect to our Flag & Country"

"No leadership in NFL!"

"Total disrespect for our great country!"

"Showed such disrespect for country!"

"Disrespecting our country"

Regarding National Football League:

"Ratings are way down"

"If the players stood proudly for our Flag and Anthem, and it is all shown on broadcast, maybe ratings could come back?"

"I just find it hard to watch, and always will, until they stand for the FLAG!"

"No escaping to Locker Rooms!"

"Stadiums that are now having a very hard time filling up"

"Hemorrhaging"

"Attendance and ratings way down"

"Too much talk, not enough action."

"Getting massive tax breaks while at the same time disrespecting our Anthem, Flag and Country"

"Ratings for NFL football are way down except before game starts, when people tune in to see whether or not our country will be disrespected!"

"The booing at the NFL football game last night, when the entire Dallas team dropped to its knees, was loudest I have ever heard. Great anger"

"Attendance and ratings are WAY DOWN"

"Boring games"

"Bad ratings!"

"Should change policy!"

On CNN Contributor, Ana Navarro:

"flunkie"

"One of the dumbest people in politics"

"Has no talent, no TV persona"

The New Hampshire Union Leader (Newspaper):

"failing"

"Won't survive"

"Highly unethical"

"Kicked out of the ABC news debate like a dog"

"Circulation dropping to record lows"

"They aren't worthy of representing the great people of NH"

"Endorsed a candidate who can't win"

"Unethical record"

"Failing"

"Stupid"

"Desperate"

"Bad management"

"Begged me for ads"

"Dying"

"Will be dead in 2 years"

"Has been run into the ground"

On New York Democrats:

"Sleazy"

On North American Free Trade Agreement
(NAFTA):

"horrendous"

"Has so badly hurt our Country"

"Old, very costly & anti-USA"

"One of the WORST Trade Deals ever made"

"Should never have been signed"

"A bad joke!"

"Worst trade deal ever made"

"A one-sided deal from the beginning"

"Worst deal in US history"

"The worst economic deal in U.S. history"

Regarding judge Brett Kavanaugh:

"What's happening to Justice Kavanaugh is a disgrace. This guy is not a good man, he is a great man. He has to go to his church with his family while these terrible reports are being written about him, a disgrace!" Dan Bongino

"I call for the Resignation of everybody at The New York Times involved in the Kavanaugh SMEAR story"

"And while you're at it, the Russian Witch Hunt Hoax, which is just as phony!"

"They've taken the Old Grey Lady and broken her down, destroyed her virtue and ruined her reputation…"

On President Barak Obama:

"gave Iran 150 Billion Dollars and got nothing"

"Had a big campaign finance violation"

"Got nowhere with North Korea"

"Did NOTHING about North Korea"

"He was in charge, not me, and did nothing"

"Cheatin' Obama"

"Why didn't he do something about Russian meddling?"

"Failed policies"

"Had zero chemistry with Putin"

"NOTHING about Russia"

"Colluded or obstructed"

"Did NOTHING after being informed in August about Russian meddling"

"A disaster!"

"Weak!"

"Terrible!"

"Had my "wires tapped" in Trump Tower just before the victory"

"A NEW LOW!"

"How low has President Obama gone to tapp my phones during the very sacred election process"

"Bad (or sick) guy!"

"He thinks he would have won against me. He should say that but I say NO WAY!"

"If Obama worked as hard on straightening out our country as he has trying to protect and elect Hillary, we would all be much better off!"

"Why is he campaigning instead of creating jobs & fixing Obamacare? Get back to work"

"Not a natural deal maker"

"Only makes bad deals!"

"Should have gone to Louisiana days ago, instead of golfing. Too little, too late!"

"Disastrous judgment"

"Perhaps the worst president in the history of the United States!"

"Doesn't have a clue"

"Trying to destroy Israel with all his bad moves"

"Living in a world of the make believe!"

"WEAK leadership"

"Failed"

"The worst president in U.S. history!"

"Weak"

"Looks and sounds so ridiculous"

"Perhaps the worst president in U.S. history!"

"Spends so much time speaking of the so-called Carbon footprint, and yet he flies all the way to Hawaii on a massive old 747"

"Is our president insane?"

"Has a horrible attitude"

"He is just so bad!"

"I did much better on 60 Minutes last week than President Obama did tonight"

"Incompetent leader"

"All talk & no action"

"Hollowing out our military"

"Weak & ineffective"

Regarding Obama Care:

"Doesn't work"

"Deductibles are far too high"

"Really bad HealthCare!"

"The cost of Obama Care is far too high for our great citizens"

"Almost worthless or unusable"

"The DEDUCTIBLE which comes with Obama Care is so high that it is practically not even useable!"

"Hurts families badly"

"An UNCONSTITUTIONAL disaster!"

"OWNED by the Democrats"

"A disaster"

"A 'product' that never had a chance of working"

"Causing such grief and tragedy for so many"

"Imploding"

"A broken mess"

"Badly broken, big premiums"

"Torturing the American People"

"Disastrous"

"Nightmare!"

"Dead"

"Failing"

"DISASTER"

"In a death spiral"

"On its last legs"

"You can't compare anything to Obama Care
because Obama Care is dead"

"Will explode"

"Horrible"

"Bad healthcare"

Regarding Bloomberg Journalist Tim O'Brien:

"dumb guy with no clue"

"Really stupid talking head"

"Ropey writer"

Regarding Forbes staff writer, Clare O'Connor,
"dummy"
"Dummy"
"Dummy writer"

On Lawrence O'Donnell of MSNBC:
"a fool"
"Dopey"
"Dopey political pundit"
"One of the dumber people on television"

On Department of Justice Official Bruce Ohr:
"How the hell is Bruce Ohr still employed at the
Justice Department?"
"A total joke!"
"A creep thinking he would get caught in a
dishonest act"

On U.S. Representative Ilhan Omar:
"Anti-Semitic, anti-Israel and ungrateful U.S.
HATE statements"
"Out of control, except for her control of
Nancy!"

On U.S. Senator Rand Paul:

"Will forever (future political campaigns) be known as 'the Republican who saved Obama Care."

"Such a negative force when it comes to fixing healthcare"

"Failed presidential candidate"

"Made a fool of himself"

"Lowly"

"Didn't get the right gene"

"Lightweight"

"Why is Rand Paul allowed to take advantage of the people of Kentucky"

"Truly weird"

"Reminds me of a spoiled brat without a properly functioning brain"

On Speaker of the House Nancy Pelosi:

"Will never be able to see or understand the great promise of our Country"

"Tearing the United States apart"

"Her leadership has passed no meaningful Legislation"

"Has lost all control of Congress"

"Getting nothing done"

"Behaved so irrationally"

"Has gone so far to the left that she has now officially become a Radical Democrat"

"So petrified of the 'lefties' □ in her party that she has lost control"

"By the way, clean up the streets in San Francisco, they are disgusting!"

"Could somebody please explain to Nancy & her "big donors"□in wine country that people working on farms (grapes) will have easy access in!"

"A wonderful person whose ideas & policies may be bad, but who should definitely be given a 4th chance"

"Trying very hard & has every right to take down the Democrat Party"

"Will Make America Weak Again!"

"Want to protect illegal immigrants far more than the citizens of our country"

"Weak on Crime and Border security"

"Did NOTHING about North Korea"

"Wanting to end the big Tax Cuts and Raise Taxes"

"Going absolutely crazy"

"Want illegal immigrants flooding into our
Country unchecked"

"Weak on Crime"

"Want to substantially RAISE Taxes"

On former Texas Governor, Rick Perry:

"Did an absolutely horrible job of securing the
border"

"Should be ashamed of himself"

"Failed on the border"

"Should be forced to take an IQ test"

"Doesn't understand what the word
demagoguery means"

"Failed at the border"

"Needs a new pair of glasses"

On Tony Podesta (prominent former lobbyist &
Democratic donor):

"A VERY well connected Democrat working in
the Swamp of Washington, D.C."

Regarding former Secretary of State Collin
Powell:

"I was never a fan"

"Weak understanding of weapons of mass destruction in Iraq"

On Puerto Rico:

"politicians are incompetent or corrupt"

"Got far more money than Texas & Florida combined, yet their government can't do anything right"

"The place is a mess - nothing works"

"All their local politicians do is complain & ask for more money"

"Polls are grossly incompetent, spend the money foolishly or corruptly, & only take from USA"

"Such bad Island leadership"

"So much money wasted"

"Massive payments, and so little appreciation!"

On Restaurant, The Red Hen:

"Should focus more on cleaning its filthy canopies, doors and windows"

"Badly needs a paint job"

"If a restaurant is dirty on the outside, it is dirty on the inside!"

On former U.S. Senator Harry Reid:

"He got thrown out"

"Working hard to put a good spin on his failed career"

"Led through lies and deception"

"Went insane"

"When he was sane, agreed with us"

On The Republican Establishment:

"Dishonest"

"Failing"

"Could not stop Obama (twice)"

"Out of self-preservation, is concerned w/ my high poll #s"

Regarding Republicans:

"very sad"

"Carried over the line on my back"

"Do very little to protect their President"

"So naive!"

"Disloyal"

"Come at you from all sides"

"Don't know how to win"

"Selfishly opposed to me!"

"Hollowing out our military"

On Mitt Romney:

"If Mitt Romney spent the same energy fighting Barack Obama as he does fighting Donald Trump, he could have won the race (maybe)!"

"Is he a Flake?"

"I won big, and he didn't"

"Really sad"

"Choked like a dog"

"A mixed up man who doesn't have a clue. No wonder he lost!"

"Failed"

"Failed presidential candidate"

"The man who 'choked' and let us all down"

"Let us all down in the last presidential race"

"A disaster candidate who had no guts and choked"

"A total joke and everyone knows it!"

"Why did Mitt Romney BEG me for my endorsement four years ago?"

"Doesn't know how to win"

"Desperate move by the man who should have easily beaten Barrack Obama"

"Failed Presidential Candidate"

"Didn't show his tax return until SEPTEMBER 21, 2012, and then only after being humiliated by Harry R"

"Bad messenger for establishment!"

"One of the dumbest and worst candidates in the history of Republican politics"

"So awkward and goofy"

"I don't need his angry advice"

"Blew an election that should have never been lost"

"Terrible 'choke' loss to Obama"

"Why would anybody listen to Mitt Romney?"

"Lost an election that should have easily been won"

On Former Deputy White House Chief of Staff, Karl Rove:

"A failed Jeb Bushy"

"Never says anything good & never will"

"Shouldn't be on the air!"

"Should be fired!"

"Sick"

"Loser"

"So biased"

"Still thinks Romney won"

"Dummy"

"No credibility"

"Fox News should can him"

"Dopey"

"Pushing Republicans down the same old path of defeat"

"Shouldn't be allowed to do [his] bias commentary"

"Establishment flunky"

"Should get a life"

"Just totally bombed"

"A loser"

"Has ZERO credibility"

"An establishment dope"

"Has made so many mistakes"

"Total fool"

"An all talk, no action dummy!"

"Part of the Republican Establishment problem"

"Purposely mischaracterized my statement"

"Moron"

"Easy to beat!"

"Spent $430 million and lost ALL races"

"Wasted $400 million"

"Didn't win one race"

"Total loser"

"A clown with zero credibility"

"Irrelevant clown, sweats and shakes nervously"

"Has zero cred"

"Made fool of himself in '12"

"A bush plant who called all races wrong"

Regarding U.S. Senator Marco Rubio:

"Bought and paid for by lobbyists!"

"Worst voting record in the U.S. Senate in many years"

"Will never MAKE AMERICA GREAT AGAIN!"

"Lightweight"

"Dishonest"

"He is scamming Florida"

"Fraud lightweight"

"Big loser"

"Failed presidential candidate"

"Rubio puts out ad that my pilot was a drug dealer- not true, not my pilot!"

"Never even shows up to vote"

"A joke!"

"Interesting how my numbers have gone so far up since lightweight Marco Rubio has turned nasty. Love it!"

"Phony"

"Treated America's ICE officers 'like absolute trash' in order to pass Obama's amnesty"

"Gave amnesty to criminal aliens guilty of 'sex offenses.' DISGRACE!"

"Just another Washington D.C. politician"

"All talk and no action"

"Little"

"Poor work ethic!"

"The lightweight no show Senator from Florida, just another Washington politician"

"The lightweight no show Senator from Florida"

"Set to be the 'puppet' of the special interest Koch brothers"

"The lightweight from Florida"

"Not as smart as Cruz, and may be an even bigger liar"

"Doesn't even show up for votes!"

"Once a choker, always a choker!"

"Mr. Meltdown"

"He is a choker, and once a choker, always a choker!"

"Looks like a little boy on stage"

"Not presidential material!"

"Lightweight choker"

"Looks like a little boy on stage"

"Not presidential material"

"Very weak on illegal immigration"

"Couldn't even respond properly to President Obama's State of the Union Speech without pouring sweat & chugging water"

"A highly overrated politician"

"Cannot be President"

"Only won the debate in the minds of desperate people"

"Very disloyal to Jeb"

"Weak on illegal immigration"

"VERY weak on illegal immigration"

"Perfect little puppet"

"Very disloyal"

"Never made ten cents"

"Totally controlled"

"Lazy"

"All talk and no action"

"Very weak on stopping illegal immigration"

"VERY weak on immigration"

"Knows nothing about finance"

"Incapable of making great trade deals"

"Will allow anyone into the country"

"Just another all talk, no action, politician"

"Truly doesn't have a clue!"

Regarding Allegations of collusion between Russia and members of the Trump campaign:

"An illegally started investigation that failed"

"An expensive and comprehensive Witch Hunt"

"PRESIDENTIAL HARASSMENT!"

"ILLEGAL Witch Hunt"

"The greatest Hoax in American History"

"A tremendous waste of time and energy"

"A sick & unlawful investigation"

"a giant SCAM"

"A Treasonous Hoax"

"The greatest con-job in the history of American Politics!"

"An illegal investigation"

"The worst and most corrupt political

"Disgraceful!"

"Hoax"

"An Illegally Started Hoax that never should
have happened"

"A total fraud on your President and the
American people!"

"The greatest Scam in political history"

"Hoax"

"Russian Collusion Delusion"

"Very few think it is legit"

"The "Insurance Policy", the biggest Scandal in
the history of our Country!"

"There was (and is) no crime. Bad!"

"Should NEVER happen to another President!"

"A big, fat, fishing expedition desperately in
search of a crime"

"PRESIDENTIAL HARASSMENT!"

"Presidential Harassment"

Regarding 60 Minutes,

"Such a "puff piece" on Nancy Pelosi by
60minutes,"

"Did a phony story about child separation"

"Fake 60 Minutes!"

"Questions were biased and slanted, the facts incorrect"

Regarding U.S. Senator Bernie Sanders:

"Crazy Bernie"

"Crazy Bernie Sanders"

"Please show a little more anger and indignation when you get screwed!"

"Crazy Bernie"

"Disaster!"

"Crazy Bernie"

"Got duped!"

"Crazy Bernie!"

"Crazy"

"Did Bernie go home and go to sleep?"

"He just wants to shut down and go home to bed!"

"Totally sold out"

"Waste of time"

"Has done such a complete fold"

"Has totally given up on his fight for the people"

"Has lost his energy and his strength"

"Flamed out"

"Exhausted"

"No energy left!"

"Exhausted"

"Just can't go on any longer"

"SAD!"

"Ending really weak"

"Has abandoned his supporters"

"Not true to himself"

"Selling out!"

"Has totally sold out"

"Crazy"

"Is lying when he says his disruptors aren't told to go to my events. Be careful Bernie, or my supporters will go to yours!"

"He would be so easy to beat!"

"Wacko"

"A disaster"

"Can't even defend his own microphone"

"Very sad!"

Regarding former U.S. Congressman Mark Sanford:

"I have never been a fan of his!"

"So bad"

"Has been very unhelpful to me in my campaign to MAGA"

"He is MIA and nothing but trouble"

"He is better off in Argentina"

On U.S. Senator Ben Sasse:

"Really sad"

"Looks more like a gym rat than a U.S. Senator"

"How the hell did he ever get elected?"

"Totally ineffective"

Regarding Saturday Night Live:

"Not funny/no talent"

"Spend all of their time knocking the same person (me), over & over, without so much of a mention of "the other side"

"An advertisement without consequences"

"Nothing funny"

"Tired"

"Total Republican hit job"

"Democrat spin machine"

"It is all nothing less than unfair news coverage and Dem commercials"

"I don't watch Saturday Night Live (even though I past hosted it)"

"No longer funny"

"No talent or charm"

"Just a political ad for the Dems"

"The worst of NBC"

"Not funny"

"Cast is terrible"

"Always a complete hit job"

"Really bad television!"

"Unwatchable!"

"Totally biased"

"Not funny"

"Sad"

"A totally one-sided, biased show - nothing funny at all"

"Boring"

"Unfunny show"

Regarding U.S Congressman Adam Schiff:

"Spent two years knowingly and unlawfully lying and leaking"

"Should be forced to resign from Congress!"

"Gone stone cold CRAZY"

"Liddle Adam Schiff"

"The leakin' monster of no control"

"Little"

"Desperate to run for higher office"

"One of the biggest liars and leakers in
Washington"

"Leaves closed committee hearings to illegally
leak confidential information"

"Must be stopped!"

"Sleazy"

"Totally biased"

"Spends all of his time on television pushing the
Dem loss excuse!"

Regarding Chuck Schumer:

"Will never be able to see or understand the
great promise of our Country"

"Cryin' Chuck"

"He's just upset that he didn't win the Senate,
after spending a fortune"

"Big fans of being weak and passive with Iran"

"No clue"

"So funny to watch Schumer groveling"

"Crying Chuck"

"Told his favorite lie"

"Had a temper tantrum"

"Very Unfair!"

"Cryin' Chuck"

"Want to protect illegal immigrants far more than the citizens of our country"

"Weak on Crime and Border security"

"Used to want Border security - now he'll take Crime!"

"Did NOTHING about North Korea"

"Weak on Crime"

"High Tax Schumer"

"Failed with North Korea and Iran"

"We don't need his advice!"

"Cryin' Chuck Schumer"

"Took such a beating over the shutdown that he is unable to act on immigration!"

"Cryin' Chuck"

"Humiliating defeat"

"Want illegal immigrants flooding into our Country unchecked"

"Want to substantially RAISE Taxes"

"Sold John McCain a bill of goods"

"So indignant"

"Total hypocrite!"

"Fake Tears Chuck Schumer"

"Clown"

Regarding the Ghost writer 'The Art of the Deal,' Tony Schwartz:

"Hardly knows me"

"Never liked his style"

"Irrelevant dope!"

"Dummy writer"

"Wanted to do a second book with me for years (I said no)"

"A hostile basket case who feels jilted!"

On Arnold Schwarzenegger:

"Isn't voluntarily leaving the Apprentice"

"Was fired by his bad (pathetic) ratings, not by me"

"Sad"

"Did a really bad job as Governor of California and even worse on the Apprentice"

"Got swamped (or destroyed) by comparison"

Former U.S. Attorney general Jeff Sessions:

"Didn't have a clue!"

"Should be ashamed of himself"

"Good job Jeff......"

"Doesn't understand what is happening underneath his command position"

"So look into all of the corruption on the "other side""

"Come on Jeff"

"So unfair Jeff, Double Standard"

"Didn't tell me he was going to recuse himself...I would have quickly picked someone else"

"VERY weak position on Hillary Clinton crimes"

Regarding actor Jussie Smollett:

"Outrageous"

"An embarrassment to our Nation!"

"Racist and dangerous comments"

Regarding Tom Stayer, a philanthropist & Environmentalist:

"Weirdo"

"Still trying to remain relevant by putting himself on ads begging for impeachment"

"Weirdo"

"Doesn't have the 'guts' or money to run for President"

"He's all talk!"

"Wacky"

"Comes off as a crazed & stumbling lunatic"

"Should be running out of money pretty soon"

"Wacky"

"Totally unhinged"

"Has been fighting me and my Make America Great Again agenda from beginning"

"Never wins elections!"

Regarding former New Hampshire Governor John Sununu:

"Dummy"

"Couldn't get elected dog catcher"

"Forgot to mention my phenomenal biz success rate"

Regarding U.S. Senator Jon Tester:

"Will vote with Cryin' Chuck Schumer and Nancy Pelosi - never with us!"

"The only thing keeping Tester alive is he has millions and millions of dollars from outside liberals and leftists"

"Says one thing to voters and does the EXACT OPPOSITE in Washington"

"Takes his orders form Pelosi & Schumer"

"Wants to raise your taxes, take away your 2A, open your borders, and deliver MOB RULE"

"Vicious and totally false statements"

"Looks to be in big trouble in the Great State of Montana!"

"Behaved worse than the Democrat Mob did with Justice K!"

"Has let the people of Montana down"

"Does not deserve another six years"

"Allegations made by Senator Jon Tester against Admiral/Doctor Ron Jackson are proving false"

"Tester should resign"

"Not fair"

"Tester should lose race in Montana"

"Very dishonest and sick!"

On Former U.S. Secretary of State:

"A man who is "dumb as a rock"

"Totally ill prepared and ill equipped to be Secretary of State"

"Made up a story (he got fired)"

"Didn't have the mental capacity needed"

"Dumb as a rock"

"I couldn't get rid of him fast enough"

"Lazy as hell"

"Wasting his time trying to negotiate with Little Rocket Man"

"Save your energy Rex"

On Meet the Press Moderator:

"Sleepy Eyes"

"A man with so little touch for politics"

"Totally one-sided interview"

"Totally biased against me"

"Sleepy eyes"

"So dishonest in his reporting"

"No ratings"

"Was going off the air until I came along"

"Very dishonest"

"Just hopeless"

"Knows so little about politics"

"Still not nice"

"I saved his job"

"Sleepy eyes"

"Will be fired like a dog"

"Love watching him fail"

"Killing Meet the Press"

"Pathetic"

Regarding the Prime Minister of Canada:

"Acts hurt when called out!"

"False statements at his news conference"

"Acted so meek and mild"

"Very dishonest & weak"

"So indignant

…And much, much more that could not be included in this writing.

Taunting by the Affluent

My Lord and my God

Won't you send me a comforter?

I have become like Job

Full of wounds and sufferings

Full of questions but no answers

I cry but you hear me not

I pray but you answer me not

I suffer but you pity me not

I look for you but you are nowhere to be found

I stretch out my hands for help but none is

forthcoming

I'm in shambles

People mock me

They laugh at me

They say I have made a deal with the devil

"She made a deal with the devil; leave her

alone," they whisper

"We have our own troubles"

"Let her deal with her own troubles"

"The devil will see her through," they say

She was cursed by God from the beginning
Leave her alone lest her curse fall upon us and
our children
They go their way despising me, cursing me
Lazy, they call me; unwilling to work they say
He lost his job because of incompetency, they
whisper among themselves about my
beloved
They laugh before me saying, "What bad
economy?"
Don't we have our jobs and health coverage?
Let him deal with his unemployment
His problems are not ours—why should we
care?
He is where he is because of his own doings
He is where he belongs

Those who would come to my rescue, they
ridicule
My helper they call a socialist
They say he is a big spender
"He takes from the rich to give to the poor,"
they accuse him
A heart of stone they have

Calling me lazy and unfit

Calling me good for nothing

Putting a label on me

Once I was with them

Once I was among them

Working hard building the land

Contributing to the success of the land just like them

These facts they choose not to remember

These facts they ignore

Now that misfortune has stricken me, they call me lazy and unfit

These people have a heart of stone

A heart of stone they have

Nonetheless, my gratitude to you who made sacrifices

Men and women of the silver screen, I salute you

The producers and writers

Composers, singers, and the commoner

For coming to my rescue; you soothed my soul

And you who prayed for me; the Lord will not forget you

May the Lord shine his light upon you and your children.

May he bless you and multiply your lot . . .

Men Behaving Inappropriately

What are you hiding?

Mr. Cosby, you who broke racial barriers in Hollywood on your way to TV superstardom as America's Dad?

You, convicted of drugging and molesting a woman in the first big celebrity trial?

Were you unfairly accused?

Say it isn't so, sir. Please tell us that it is all a mistake.

Mr. Weinstein, a name so renown and synonymous with the silver screen, why are you charged with rape in the first and third degrees, as well as criminal sexual act in the first degree for forcible sexual acts against innocent women who trusted you?

Why the abuse of power?

Why the betrayal of so much trust?

Predators in prison will now take turns exploiting you.

They will now take delight in doing what you did to all those innocent women.

And you, Dr. Nassar, we trusted you with our youngsters. Our youngsters trusted you to do the right thing. Why the betrayal? Sexually harassing female students and pressuring them for nude selfies.
You too will now be pressured into sexual acts, Sexual acts by your cellmates.
Kevin Spacey, you who shone on the silver screen but a pervert all along.
 Why did you make sexual advances on another man?
Why did you make sexual advances on Anthony Rapp when he was only 14?
Did you not consider that he was underage?
Why did you not direct your pervasion towards men of your own age and interest?

And you Senator Moore, betraying the trust of your constituents, have you no shame?
Disguising yourself as a political & religious zealot while preying upon underage girls all

those years, did you not think of the
consequences?

Hell awaits your kind with open arms.

A rising Democratic star, fallen, Mr. Franken
the senator, you of all people doing despicable
acts.

Oh, how the mighty are fallen.

Mr. Chef and chief restaurateur Batali, you who
sizzled and dazzled us with you gifts in the
kitchen, what is with all the rampant sexual
harassment against your employees?

Could you not go about your sexual exploits the
right way?

Mr. Gary Goddard, the theater prodigy, those
young child actors looked upon you as a director
& mentor, why betray their trust?

Those who trusted you now accuse you of
molestation and or attempted molestation of
them.

"This is a man who's attracted to little boys, and
attracted in the sickest way," says Edwards.

"This is not love; this is not friendship what he was doing," cries out one of your victims.

"It was horror because it is manipulating young hearts and minds," adds another.

Those were young & innocent boys you molested, you wench.

Your day too, will come in court.

You too will feel the pain of molestation when justice is served & you are locked up for your crimes.

Franco, why is your behavior inappropriate or sexually exploitative toward women?

In your presence, why did women say "we feel there was an abuse of power, and a culture of exploiting non-celebrity women, and a culture of women being replaceable."

As a celebrity, did you use your influence to intimidate and take advantage of women?

Classical musician James Levine, you who were designated by the Metropolitan Opera as a towering figure in classical music, why were you fired?

Were the evidence found against you for sexual abuse and harassment true?
Could you not go about the 'dating business' the right way?

Investor Michael Ferro, making unwanted sexual advances toward women, have you no shame at all?
Could you not use your skills in investments to invest in women the proper way?
Or did you view women as merely stocks?

Stan Lee of Marvel Comics, you are 95 years old but acted like a teenager.
During a professional massage when Carballo massaged your quadriceps, why did you behave like a young boy moaning and groaning?
Why did you grab Carballo's foot and touch it to your penis and scrotum?
Have you no regard for women?
Do you lack self-respect?
Why did you inappropriately grab her during a massage?

What were you hiding behind those Marvel
Comics?

R. Kelly, it is you again.
Why the longstanding allegations of sexual
abuse by you?
Why the sexual exploitation of the young and
innocent?
Why the deviant and lecherous behavior?

Why do some men in power misbehave?
Why do some men in positions of influence
misbehave?

Made in the USA
Columbia, SC
28 October 2022

70128390R00095